I Have Been Blessed

By Beatrice Parker

Scripture taken from the King James Version of the Holy Bible, which is in the public domain.

Cover image: istockphoto.com/sutlafk

ISBN: 9798372762381

Table of Contents

Dedication

I have always wanted to write a book about my life, beginning with my childhood, to when I was hit by a semi-truck at age three and pronounced dead, all the way to age seventy-five with the passing of my husband after fifty-three years of marriage. I now have something to pass down to succeeding family generations and to encourage others in their journeys, as well.

I want to dedicate the book to my husband, Rudolph, for all the things he imparted in my life, our sons' lives, and members of his church.

Dedication

Chapter 1
My Early Life

I was born in 1946 to Frank Keary Washington, Sr., and Callie Mae Washington, in Burlington, Vermont, about six hours from New York. I am the third of seven children. After my two older siblings were born in Philadelphia, Pennsylvania, my parents; the two siblings; my grandparents; and my aunt and uncle, and cousin, left there to come to Vermont to work in the woolen mills. Their job was to help process wool so it could be used to make clothing. I assume it was the best job they could get in those days since I always heard them talk about how glad they were to be working in the mills.

My brothers, sisters, and I grew up in a predominantly white, middle-class neighborhood where everyone owned their own home and had a car. There was plenty of African-American culture in New York, but we had never visited there, so we were unaware of it until the "Fresh Air Kids" would get bussed into our town every summer to live with different families so we could all fully experience one another's lives for that short period.

I grew up during the time of segregation, though it probably affected our parents, grandparents, and other extended family members more than it affected us as children, especially considering the adults in our family were born in Alabama. But we were just children growing up, playing with our white friends, and having fun doing things we shouldn't be doing, getting caught, and blaming one another, just like every other kid in the world.

My sister, Pat, was the oldest, and she was like a mother to us, but we didn't pay much attention to her orders. My older brother, Frank, was always doing his own thing. So, I mostly hung out with my two younger brothers, Lewis and Tony; two younger sisters, Callie and Stephanie; and my cousin, Alice. Alice was in the same grade I was even though she was a year older. Our birthdays are also in the same month. Mine is on the 17th and hers is on the 24th. We still keep in touch, and I try to get to see her every time I visit Vermont.

When we were kids, we spent our winter days roller- and ice skating together, having snowball fights, and making snowmen, and our summer days getting ice cream at the Dairy Queen, swimming in Lake Champlain or playing in the park. When we went to Lake Champlain, Frank would always tell me "Don't go out too deep, because you know you can't swim very well," but I ignored him and went out to where the water was up to my waist. One day when I was about thirteen, a big wave came and knocked me off my feet. I tried to stand back up again, but I kept going under. Miraculously, I felt some arms pulling me up. It was my brother, Frank. He scolded me all the way to shore. Needless to say that never happened again.

I was a quiet and shy kid in school, though, so my interactions were limited to family members and a couple of close friends, like Alice, and my best friend, Beatrice Hill, who I ate lunch with all the time. I think we were best friends because we had the same first name, we were both quiet and shy, and we were both on the honor roll. I was one of those rare kids who was good at both English and math.

I also had a white boyfriend, named Mark Hill (no relation to Beatrice), in the sixth grade, though we made a pact that we wouldn't tell anyone we were together. I don't know if it was because he was white and I was African-American or because we just didn't want to be teased.

I never went to any social events, like the high school prom. I got in trouble only once when I was in grade school, because my mother had put my hair in curls and one of my classmates touched them and I hollered, "Don't touch my hair!" Our teacher told me I was rude because the classmate just wanted to touch the curls, but I didn't get punished. I was just embarrassed.

By Beatrice Parker

Chapter 2
The Day I Died and Came Back to Life

One day when I was three, my mother was busy working in the kitchen. I didn't see any of my brothers and sisters around, so I sneaked outside to look for them. Once I got outside, I saw them walking through the ally across the street, licking popsicles. When they saw me, they put the popsicles behind their backs, but I had already seen what they had in their hands.

Without looking to see if there was any traffic coming, I darted into the street as a semitruck was coming around the corner at full speed. The driver couldn't stop in time and his truck hit me. I wasn't aware of what had happened until I discovered my spirit was hovering outside my body and above the crowd that had gathered at the accident scene.

I saw my mother coming out of the house, and I heard her screaming. Mr. Rome, who owned the mom-and-pop store on the corner, was shaking his head and saying, "What a shame." I was pronounced dead, but my mother wasn't having it, so she started praying in tongues that her child would live and demanded the paramedics take me to the hospital. Meanwhile, I was trying to tell everyone on the ground that I was hovering over them and that I was okay, but they couldn't hear me.

God honored my mother's prayers and returned my spirit to my body, though to this day I can still see my spirit hovering over the crowd.

I stayed for six months in the hospital with my godly mother sending prayers from my beside to my Heavenly Father, who was watching over me. She told me I was wrapped halfway around the tire and had incurred two broken arms, two broken legs, and a burn on my left arm from the hot tire, so I spent the six months hanging in a sling over the hospital bed.

The Lord had mercy on me because I was still alive. Plus, I didn't incur any damage to my organs or my brain, and I don't remember experiencing any pain. The Lord blocked all that trauma from my mind, though I had to wear a shoe with a lift because one leg was shorter than the other, and I had an ugly burn scar on my left arm. But when I was five years old, I walked into kindergarten, whole and healthy, ready to meet the world as I was holding my mother's hand.

I've been having spiritual encounters ever since the Lord placed my spirit back into my body. Like many houses in Vermont, our house had squares cut out near the top of the walls to let the heat flow from room to room. One day I was playing with my dolls and I looked up and saw two brown, hairy "imps" peering at me through one of the square cut-outs. They were leaning on their elbows and watching me, but I didn't pay much attention to them. I just continued playing.

Later that day, as my mother and I were walking to the store, I guess she sensed something behind us, because we turned around and saw those imps following us. She stomped her foot and said, "Leave us alone. Stop following us." To my surprise, they obeyed her. As we turned at the corner, they disappeared and I never saw them again.

I'm also more spiritually aware in general. I know, for example, when God is telling me something that I need to pay attention to. It's as though my spirit says, "Stop and hear the voice of the Lord." When I was about eight or nine, I was folding clothes in my room, and the Lord called out to me from the corner of the room, and I said, "Yes, Lord?" As I've thought about that encounter over the years, I thought it was strange that even though there were seven of us in the family I happened to be the only one in the bedroom. I know God planned it that way.

When I was in my teens, I started becoming aware that the Lord was talking to me through prayer and my reading of the Word. When someone is preaching, my spirit will quicken to what the preacher is saying. The Lord has also reminded me many times in prayer that it was not my time to go. He sent my spirit back into my body because He had plans for me.

One day the Lord told me, "I saw you in your mother's womb, I saw you when the accident occurred, I saw you in the hospital, and I saw you when you started kindergarten. I have always been with you. I heard you praying as you lay in bed, looking out the window and up at the stars when you were a child. Didn't I answer all your prayers?

Remember when you were in your room, folding your clothes, and I called to you out loud from the corner of your room, and you replied 'Yes, Lord?' because you knew who I was without asking."

As I grew older, I had many more encounters with the Lord when I felt His Spirit speaking directly to me. These experiences always pertain to what is going on in my life at that time.

Chapter 3
My Testimony of Salvation

I grew up in the Pentecostal church, the only Black congregation in Burlington. I loved every bit of it. My mother gave me a little white Bible when I was a young girl, and we went to church Sunday mornings and Sunday nights, as well as Tuesdays and Thursdays.

By the time I was six years old, God had given me the ability to teach, without any help from my parents. My mom had her hands full, taking care of the home, and my dad went to church only once in a while. So, I started teaching Sunday school lessons to other kids my age. I taught them the stories I'd read in the little white Bible my mother had given me: Jonah and the whale, Noah and the ark, and David and Goliath. I also gave my students Bible verses to memorize, like John 3:16: "For God so loved the world, that he gave his only begotten Son, that whosoever believeth in him should not perish, but have everlasting life."

I also loved "Youth Night," which was part of every Sunday evening service. There would be a chair up front in the sanctuary for any of the youth who were brave enough to answer questions about the Bible, posed by members of the congregation. I answered all the questions correctly every time.

But even though I had been reading, teaching, and memorizing verses from the Bible, and even though I knew all the answers to all the questions I'd ever been asked on Youth Night, I didn't come to know the Lord until I was twelve because that's when I really understood what being a Christian was about. I was saved while my mother and I were watching the Christian television programs that were airing at the time. Oral Roberts and Rex Humbard were popular then.

I spent the rest of my childhood just growing up, going to school, and experiencing life, though when I was a teenager, I did read the Greatest Story Ever Told, about the life of Christ. I couldn't put it down.

One day, we showed up at church and found it padlocked. It had been taken over by another pastor who had bought it for himself and his family to use as their private home. So, we started attending First Baptist Church.

Chapter 4
My Family

By this point, my dad had left the woolen mills and started doing construction jobs. Then tragedy struck when I was a senior in high school: my father was on a building project and a huge boulder rolled on him and crushed him to death. He was just fifty years old. My mother was left with seven children, ages thirteen to nineteen, to raise on her own.

At that time, I was making top grades, landing me on the honor roll many times. So,

I was selected to be an intern at a local bank and was able to help my mother pay our family's expenses. My sister, Pat, had started her career in nursing, and my brother, Frank, worked construction, like my father did. So, they pitched in on the household bills, as well. My younger siblings, Callie, Stephanie, and Tony were too young to work.

My brother, Lewis, decided to enlist in the Vietnam War and was killed in action at the age of twenty. He and I were what they call "Irish Twins," which means we were born twelve months apart. I was born on the seventeenth and he was born on the tenth of the month, so each year we would be the same age for a week.

Callie and Stephanie have families of their own now. Patricia, who is now the matriarch of the family, is seventy-eight and lives in Vermont. When she was younger, she had four kids, three sons and one daughter. Two of her sons, Junior and Derrick, have passed away, but her other son, Thomas, lives in Vermont, and her daughter, Joyce, lives in Sacramento. Pat loves to shop, and her jewelry collection is amazing. She loved my husband dearly and always called him her pastor.

Frank is the patriarch of the family. He still lives in Vermont with his friend, Debbie. He takes antique cars and restores them into beauties. Because he had lived in Burlington for seventy-one years, in 2017 Bill Keogh and Joey Donovan, hosts of a local television station, invited him to be featured on an episode of "Stump the Chumps," where they discussed Burlington families "with all those kids." It aired on January 9, 2018, in Burlington.

Callie is seventy-three and a widow. She resides in California. She had a stroke five years ago and is working on improving her health.

Stephanie also lives in California. She is married to a man named Rudolph, which was also my husband's name. She is seventy-two and has three children: Sabrina, Rudolph Jr (Tom Tom), and Calvin.

Tony passed away on September 3, 2020, from liver cancer. He was never married and had no children. He was the kindest and most generous person you'd ever want to meet. He would give you the shirt off his back. I miss him. My niece, Joyce, and I led him to the Lord before he passed, so we will see him in heaven.

Chapter 5
Meeting My Husband

After I'd worked at the bank for two years, I moved to New York. Callie had moved there and wanted me to meet the brother of the guy she was dating. His name was Rudolph. I can truly say he was tall, dark, and handsome. It was love at first sight. He sang and played guitar and piano in a band, and I would always go with him to watch and listen to his rock-and-roll and jazz music.

We started dating when I was nineteen. Sometimes we would go to the Hudson River.

Since I'd almost drowned in Lake Champlain, I didn't like to venture out too deep. So, I just waded in the water while Rudolph swam. One day while we were down at the Hudson River, Rudolph picked me up and threw me in the water. The water wasn't deep, but I didn't like being thrown in and I told him so. After I calmed down, I explained to him why I didn't like to swim, and of course, he apologized. We also liked to visit Vermont and go with his mom and uncle to New York City. He took me to the country where he grew up and told me all about the fun he had as a kid.

His mother had given him a guitar, so he would go into the woods, stand on his favorite rock, play the guitar, and sing. He had a beautiful voice. He also had eleven siblings to play tag, kickball, and hide-and-seek with and help their father pick apples with during the apple season. At Christmas, they would chop down trees to sell.

In June 1969, Rudolph was drafted into the Army and released in September of that same year, due to a deformity in both of his wrists. After the Army gave him his discharge papers and a ticket home, a week later they showed up at the door and told him he was AWOL (Absent Without Leave) because he didn't show up for roll call that morning. When Rudolph told him he had been discharged, the Army claimed they had no record of it. So, the Army sent him to prison.

We couldn't afford an attorney, so we had to wait three months for the Army to clear up the gross mistake they had made because back then there were no computers or technology to speed things along. When the Army finally located Rudolph's discharge papers and the record of his ticket home, they gave him an honorable discharge and an apology. He wasn't bitter about the experience. In fact, he wrote a Christmas musical for the inmates while he was in prison.

Chapter 6
Marriage and Family

Rudolph and I were married on October 25, 1969, when we were both twenty-two. We lived in a middle-class apartment complex in Newburgh, fifty miles from New York City. Rudolph wasn't a Christian when we got married, but he would come to church with me. He said he didn't grow up in the church and that he and his family just went to a Catholic church sometimes. He asked a lot of questions, though.

Turns out, he'd also had an out-of-body experience when he was a child. He had a high fever and he was lying in his mother's lap when his spirit left his body. He told me he was in the air, watching his mother wrap him in garlic to draw out the fever. After that, he said he felt as though he had a calling on his life.

One day at church he finally accepted the Lord. He said he was glad he met me because he didn't know whether he would have ever come to know the Lord otherwise.

We still "dated" each other even after we were married. We would go on weekend trips to San Francisco or Lake Tahoe. Sometimes we'd go on a picnic at Folsom Lake. On Fridays we would go to the movies and out to dinner. On Thursday nights, we would pray and study the Bible together at home. The date nights and Bible studies continued even after we had our children.

We started our family not long after we were married. We returned to Vermont for awhile, and that's where our first child, Rudy,

Jr., was born. He was quiet like I was when I was a child, and he was always trying to be the big brother. He also got into trouble, just like my family, friends, and I did when we were kids. All my kids did. Once Rudy, Jr., sneaked out the window and went to a party. His brothers told me about it, and I was waiting with a switch for him to come home. I'm sure he got into other mischief I don't care to know about.

Once we returned to New York, we had two more sons, Randy and Ricky. Randy, our middle son, was a little rebellious at times, always wanting his way. So Dad would have to step in with some discipline.

Ricky, the youngest, was very kind-hearted. One day I noticed the peanut butter and jelly in our cabinet wasn't lasting as long as it usually did. In fact, it was disappearing really fast. When I mentioned it to the boys, Ricky admitted he was feeding his friends peanut butter and jelly sandwiches after school because they were hungry. Well, we had to put a stop to it even though we told him it was a kind gesture.

Our fourth child, Riley, was born at home and died soon after. I was home alone and started having pains. I didn't realize they were birth pains because he wasn't due for another month. But sure enough, out he came. He was breathing, and his little mouth was opening and closing. I wrapped him up and went downstairs to call the ambulance so we could get him to the hospital, but little Riley died before we could get there. So, we will see him in heaven.

After seven years in New York, while our sons were still children, we moved to an apartment in Sacramento in 1979. I quickly found employment at a credit union because of all my experience in banking. After a year as a teller, I was promoted to a supervisor's position and became the head of a branch with the title of Assistant Vice President. My husband left the band behind in New York and worked the carpet business.

We had been living in California for about three years when my mother came to visit. I met her when she got off the plane and was shocked to see how skinny she was. She saw the look on my face, and that was when I found out she had cancer. She hugged me and told me she loved me. She stayed for about a week before she returned home.

About a year later, I received a call from my brother, who told me that my dear beloved mother had passed. I was watching Rex Humbard, who had just finished quoting Revelation 21:4: "God shall wipe away all tears from their eyes, there shall be no more death neither shall there be any more sorrow nor crying nor pain for the former things have passed away." I thought about the little white Bible my mother had given me and how we would watch Oral Roberts and Rex Humbard. I dropped to my knees and started sobbing. Then I heard the Lord say, "Comfort yourself with my words from Revelation."

Chapter 7
My Baptism in the Holy Spirit

When we moved to California, at first we started attending a First Baptist Church like we had in New York, and we were assigned to teach the four- and five-year-olds. We were teaching them to pray, but the pastor told us to stop because he felt they couldn't understand what they were doing at their age. So we left the First Baptist Church and went to a Word of Faith church, but we didn't agree with the prosperity teaching. We finally ended up at the Assemblies of God where we stayed for seven years.

When I was thirty-four, I received the baptism of the Holy Spirit at home. The pastor of our church asked everyone who wanted to receive the baptism of the Holy Spirit to come to the altar. The elders kept praying over me with no results. Finally, they told me to go home and I would probably get it.

Sure enough, that week I was baptized in the Holy Spirit. I started speaking in tongues, which I had never done before. My husband was at work at the time, so I called and told him. He said he already knew it because the Holy Spirit had revealed it to him.

I became the women's Bible teacher at our church, which meant organizing and holding women's conferences, during which I would speak and teach workshops. My husband and I also started a counseling ministry, where I used my gift of discernment.

Chapter 8
Good Memories

We had a lot of memorable family times while our three other boys were growing up. They loved to go swimming, so they were always at someone's pool. Sometimes we'd pack a picnic lunch and spend the day at Folsom Lake. Rudolph and I even vacationed in Hawaii four times. Maui was our favorite island.

When the boys were older, my husband took up golf with some local pastors and the boys started playing shortly thereafter. I even took lessons so we could play as a family. We all loved to play. My husband even took us to the world-famous Pebble Beach in Monterey, California, but it was too expensive for us to play golf there. So we went across the street and played on the small pebble beach course. Good memories.

Rudy, Jr., played basketball in high school, just like his father did, and enlisted in the Army after he graduated. The day the recruiter came to the house to pick him up, his dad, his two brothers, and I stood on the door steps and cried as he waved from the car when they were driving away. Four years later, he was discharged from the Army and came home, got married, and started his family. His daughter, Keriko, is thirty-four years old. As of this writing, he is fifty-five years old, lives in Sacramento, and works from home doing online billing for a medical agency.

Randy played football as a running back in high school and several colleges offered him scholarships. He accepted one but was injured at practice, so his football career was over before it began. He married his high school sweetheart and had a beautiful little girl, Denne, our first grandchild, who is now thirty-two years old, and has four children (our great grandchildren): A'Riyah, who is thirteen; Artise III, who is ten; Aubrieann, who is four; and Aavi, who is three.

Randy also has two sons, Randy, Jr., who is twelve and just like his dad because he makes everyone laugh, and Rashon, who is eleven. Randy is fifty-one, lives in Sacramento with his family, and works as a non-emergency medical transport driver.

Ricky graduated high school and went to San Diego State. After he graduated, he was drafted as a tight end by the Chicago Bears. A playmate stepped on his knee during practice, and he was let go before he had the opportunity to play his first game, but he was picked up by the Jacksonville Jaguars where he played for a year. He then played in the Arena Football League before retiring. He is forty-eight, lives in Georgia, and does some sports counseling for youth. He has one son, Ricky, Jr., who is twenty-nine, and two grandchildren (our great grandchildren): Rehlanii, who is three; and Rubee, who is a year old.

Chapter 9
Starting Our Church

One day, my husband came home and told me the Lord was calling him to start a church. I wasn't thrilled about it because I had noticed in almost every church I'd been to that the pastor's wife was not happy. To make sure I didn't end up just another unhappy pastor's wife, I obeyed God and came into agreement with Rudolph as my husband to start a Pentecostal church called Christian Worship International in 1986. It wasn't easy, but I enjoyed it. I've never had any regrets.

Rudolph taught Sunday school for the adults and counseled people during the week. I taught Sunday school for the children, and the youth pastor taught the youth. We held sporting events in the park such as baseball, basketball, and swimming to evangelize, and we had a tent set up for anyone who wanted prayer or counseling. The children's Bible teacher also held activities for the kids. Our church also held mid-week Bible studies. Other pastors in the city would hold monthly meetings to support one another, and sometimes they would have one big meeting in one of the larger churches to get together and fellowship.

Rudolph's office hours were Monday, Tuesday, and Thursday from nine to five when I got off work. If we were going to have a special event like a picnic for the church or a visiting speaker, we would have the planning meeting in the evening so that those who were involved in the planning could come after work.

We had a vibrant, active, and gifted congregation, with many people getting saved and joining our local assembly. Over time, we'd built up about 150 on the rolls, with 100 showing up on Sundays. We held healing services on Sunday nights. One weekend, a woman who had been at my women's conference came to our service and asked if we would pray for the Lord to heal her of cancer. So, we prayed for her healing and she left. The following week, she came back joyful because her doctor told her she was now cancer-free. She attended our church for a few more weeks and then we never saw her again.

I was also serving as president of the local Women's Aglow ministry, which has chapters that have monthly meetings all over the world. One year, the vice president of our chapter and I attended the yearly conference in Washington, DC. On the way home, I fell asleep on the plane and had a dream. I saw screaming women falling into a fiery black pit, their skin peeling off as they scraped against the sides. In the dream, the Lord asked me three times if I would help Him, and I said that I would. Then a ladder appeared and the women were climbing out of the pit with their hands raised in praise to the Lord. He was asking me to help save the souls of women.

Both of us operated the church while taking care of our family and studying for theology degrees. It was hard work, but it all paid off. Rudolph received his Bachelor's of Theology degree from Pacific Coast Bible College in 1987, his Master's of Theology degree from Pacific Coast Bible College in 1988, and his Doctor of Ministry degree from Friends International Christian University in 1997. The same year he received his doctorate, I completed my Master's of Religious Education degree from Friends International Christian University.

Rudolph wrote his theses on the Holy Spirit. Everything in his life was about the Holy Spirit. He loved operating in the Spirit and always read everything he could about the Spirit. He loved laying his hands on people for healing, prophesying, and baptism in the Spirit.

Unfortunately, about thirty-five years into our marriage, like many church leaders, we became so engrossed in the church that our marriage started to suffer. We weren't spending time together like we used to, and the date nights stopped.

In fact, we hardly talked to each other, and when we did, we were always arguing. We stopped praying together or having our own Bible study at home. Sometimes we were so exhausted when we came home from the church that we just went to bed.

Rudolph and I started talking about divorce and separated for a while and the church lost members. But we prayed day and night, and God turned our marriage back into the strong, healthy union it had been, with Him in the center.

Chapter 10
Our Jail Ministry

One lady from our local jail ministry had started coming to church. She accepted the Lord and became a member. She met her husband there, as well, and Rudolph married them and they had a little boy. Soon, Rudolph and I became involved in the jail ministry and took the necessary classes to become prison chaplains so we could minister to prisoners in other parts of the state. In the end, we were involved in prison ministry for ten years.

I remember going to the women's jail to do an Easter service. When our group arrived at the jail, the Chaplain said she needed someone to minister to a group of women who were on their way to prison and could not be with the main population. Since I was the leader, I volunteered to do the Easter Bible study for them. I remember thinking, *You have to be ready in and season and out of season.*

As the Chaplain and I were walking to the area where I was to minister, she reminded me about the "no hostage rule," which meant if I were taken hostage, there would be no negotiating. So I said, "The Lord will take care of me." And we both smiled.

Once we got to the room, the Chaplain introduced me to the group of women and said she would be back in an hour. She left and locked us in. Normally a guest speaker would sit at the door in case she had to make a quick exit, but my chair was up front. So I walked up front, sat in the chair, and smiled. I asked them their names and told them it was a privilege to minister to them.

Then I told them the Easter Story, the Good News. Jesus loves us so much that He left the splendor of His perfect home in Heaven to come as a man to this far-from-perfect world to love far-from-perfect people, identify with us, and become our friend and companion through life. Being God, Jesus knows each of us better than anyone else who's ever walked this earth, and He and wants a personal relationship with us regardless of what we have done.

Romans 3:23 teaches us that all of us in all walks of life, whether we've been to prison or not, have sinned and fall short of the glory of God. So, none of us are better than another. Since God is perfect, our sins actually break our fellowship with the Lord. Romans 6:23 teaches us that we deserve the death penalty for our sins, but Romans 5:8 tells us that Jesus Christ went to the cross to die in our place, thus paying the death penalty for us.

If not for Jesus Christ dying for us in our place, none of us would have any hope of having our relationship with God restored here on earth or after we pass from this life into the next.

But Jesus loves us and doesn't want us to spend eternity separated from God, so He made a way for us to be reconciled with Him, free from the penalty of everything we've ever done wrong. Once we come into agreement with Jesus that we need to turn from our sins and follow Him, He releases us from the death penalty, because He paid it for us on the cross.

From that point on, we can walk in newness of life for all eternity, which is the meaning behind the resurrection. For after Jesus paid our sin debt on the cross, He spent three days and three nights in the grave, and then He rose from the dead and gave us a new beginning. We can now live knowing that we have been set free from our sins and that they will no longer have power over us because when we follow Christ, He renews our minds, giving us the ability to make different choices than we did before we came to Him.

That's what the Holy Spirit does for us.

For after we repent of our sins and come to know Christ, He sends His Holy Spirit into our hearts to comfort us, teach us, and guide us through life. John 14:16-17 calls Him our Comforter and the Spirit of Truth.

Even with Christ in our hearts, however, we are still not perfect people, so the Holy Spirit also convicts us when we do something wrong. Then we can go to God and tell Him what we did wrong and ask His forgiveness, according to 1 John 1:9, which He gives in abundance.

All we have to do to begin this wonderful journey of eternal life with Christ is to go to Him in prayer, tell Him we want a life that's different from the one we're living now, and ask Him to come into our hearts to be our leader and comforter through life. Romans 10:9 says that if we confess with our mouths that Jesus is Lord and believe in our hearts that God raised Him from the dead, we will be saved.

Before long the women started asking questions. Some had smiles on their faces.

Other just sat and listened. The hour went so fast. The Chaplain returned, and as I got up to leave, some of the women gave me a hug, even though they weren't supposed to, but the Chaplain allowed it that day. I heard some say, "Thank you."

As the Chaplain and I walked back to the rest of the group, she asked, "How did it go?"

I replied, "God is good. Everything went smooth."

Chapter 11
Rudolph's Ministry in the Community

Rudolph, along with his friend, Robert Creel, who is now deceased, and a couple of other men, were always looking for ways to minister to different groups. In 2006, Rudolph completed the Federal Bureau of Investigation's Citizens Academy Program so he could minister to men and women in the FBI.

Also, a lot of the local veterans were living on the streets or in the missions because they were alcohol or drug addicts. So, Rudolph and his friends started a ministry called Veterans for Christ, which provided clothing, transportation to the VA hospital and the grocery store, and help with paperwork so the veterans could get their benefits. The ministry also held Bible studies, gave counseling, and provided rides to church. On Sunday afternoons, they held church services at the hospitals or the missions.

Rudolph and Mr. Creel also went to the state capitol in Sacramento, asked permission to minister to the senators, and were given the OK to start a ministry to hold Bible studies with them, pray with them, and encourage them. One time when Rudolph was at the capitol, he was getting on the elevator and saw one of the senators whom he knew was on his way to prison. Rudolph heard the Holy Spirit tell him to pray for the senator, which he did, and the senator thanked him for his prayers.

Chapter 12
My Husband's Passing

Rudolph started having health problems when he was sixty. First, he was diagnosed with diabetes and started using insulin. He was doing okay until ten years later when he was diagnosed with Stage 2 kidney disease, put on medicine, and monitored by his doctor. Within five years his disease had progressed to Stage 5. He was put on dialysis and had both legs amputated. He suffered two strokes and a heart attack, and he was losing his eyesight and hearing.

After two years of his body being ravaged with disease, he was no longer able to minister outside the home. So, we started a home-based Bible study and counseling ministry. He received a couple of other ministry opportunities, as well. A pastor of another local church asked him to do a Bible study for them and to minister some Sundays. A leader of another fellowship asked him to come and minister with him. Sadly, he continued to grow weaker until he could no longer do the Bible study.

When it was nearing the time for him to pass from this life and into the loving arms of his Lord and Savior Jesus Christ, the boys and I began sitting with him day and night. We talked to him, read scripture, and just spent that time loving him. One day, I heard these lyrics from the song Beula Land on the radio: "There's just a few more days to labor and then I'll take my heavenly flight." My spirit leapt inside me, and I heard the Holy Spirit say, "That is for your husband. He has finished the work the Lord called him to do."

One night, I was lying beside him. He had been sleeping for ten days. I fell asleep and woke up. I looked at him and called his name. His eyes flew open and he looked at me. I told him "I love you." He made a little smile, his face glowed, and the room lit up. Then he closed his eyes and passed into glory. God had taken his servant home. He had finished His work the Lord had called him to do, just like the Holy Spirit told me.

I laid my head on his chest and wept softly. My husband of fifty-three years, my friend, my lover, the father of my children, was in eternity. He was seventy-five years old. One day, I will join him in heaven in endless praise to our Lord Jesus Christ, without being hindered by age or disease, and I look forward to that day.

The funeral was not just about grieving; it was also about worship and praise to our glorious heavenly Father for my husband's ministry here on earth. It was broadcast on Zoom so that those who were not able to attend could see it. The turnout was huge and included all the local pastors he had fellowshipped with in ministry. Fifteen people spoke at the service. They talked about how his counseling ministry helped them get through difficult times and how they will see him again on the other side. One pastor said that everyone who knew him and loved him was thankful for the experience.

The Honorable Richard Pan of the 6th Senatorial District of California issued a beautiful Resolution commemorating my husband's work with the senators. It is in a beautiful gold frame:

A MEMORIAL RESOLUTION
By the Honorable Richard Pan,
6th Senatorial District
Relative to Memorializing

WHEREAS, the passing on September 3, 2022, of Elk Grove resident Dr. Rudolph G. Parker has been met with great sadness tempered by profound gratitude for a life well lived, a life exemplified by his compassion, loyalty, and commitment to his family, his community, and his friends, which caused those who knew him to be better for the experience and the people of the State of California to be served wisely, selflessly, spiritually; and

WHEREAS, A man of understanding, wisdom, strength, and patience who was always ready to extend the hand of friendship and open his heart, Dr. Rudy Parker was born on August 14, 1947, in Newburgh, New York, and relocated in 1979 to Sacramento, California, where he became Pastor of Christian Worship International Christian University in 1997, in addition to successfully completing the Federal Bureau of Investigation's Citizens Academy Program in 2006; and

WHEREAS, Dr. Parker ministered to California State Assembly Members and Senators for many years at the California State Capitol, including engaging in weekly spiritual meetings with legislators where he offered prayer and words of encouragement, and he also was a part of the National Day of Prayer at the State Capitol and participated in many prayer marches and events; and

WHEREAS, A man of great compassion, Dr. Parker additionally led a prison ministry that ministered to inmates at state prisons in Folsom, Vacaville, and Susanville and at the Sacramento County Jail; and

WHEREAS, an accomplished musician who learned to play the piano and guitar, Dr. Parker also enjoyed golf-both playing and observing-and was able to play at one of his favorite courses in Pebble Beach, and over the years he and his wife of 52 years, Beatrice M. Parker, also traveled to his favorite destination, Hawaii, and visited their favorite cities of Monterey, San Francisco, and Lake Tahoe; and

WHEREAS, for all of his professional life as a pastor, Dr. Rudolph Parker provided compassionate and wise spiritual leadership to the community and was a shining example of the great good that can be accomplished by one dedicated and moral individual, and he leaves to mourn his six sisters and one brother; and a host of aunts, cousins, nieces, nephews and extended family members; now, therefore, be it

RESOLVED BY SENATOR RICHARD PAN, that he joins the family and friends of Dr. Rudolph G. Parker in celebrating and revering the accomplishments and legacy of a distinguished and caring individual who lived life to the fullest, whose generosity was extended to everyone without hesitation or expectation of reward, and whose spirit will live forever in the hearts and memories of all his loved ones.

After the funeral, we held a repass in our home with all our loved ones gathering and talking about their memories of my husband. Once everyone left, I laid down to rest. As I was drifting off to sleep, I heard my husband call my name. I turned to see where the voice was coming from, and I heard him call me again. Then in my spirit I heard God say, "Everything is okay."

Then He said, "Remember the dream I gave you of screaming women falling into a fiery black pit, their skin peeling off as they scraped against the sides? I asked you three times if you would help me. You said you would. Then suddenly as you watched, a ladder appeared and the women were climbing out of the pit with their hands raised praising the Lord." It is time to fulfill that vision. You have come to a bend in the road, and I am around the bend waiting for you. Pick up your cross and follow me."

Our church is no longer in operation, but we did keep it in good status as a 301 C so I could continue to carry the cross of ministering to women through Bible studies, conferences, and counseling under Beatrice Parker Ministries. I will continue carrying that cross until I walk into the presence of the Lord and see Him face to face. I also attend another church operated by some friends of mine and we fellowship together.

Endnote
I Have Been Blessed

It has been seventy-five years and "I Have Been Blessed." Michael Compton wrote a song with that title that reflects my thoughts perfectly. God has been so good to me. There's no way I can count the number of times He has thought of me over the past seventy-five years or the number of blessings He has bestowed upon me. I just continue to thank Him for the eternal lovingkindness He has shown my family and me.